Six Sigma
Project Management:
A Pocket Guide

Also Available from ASQ Quality Press:

Six Sigma for the Shop Floor: A Pocket Guide
Roderick A. Munro

*Customer Centered Six Sigma: Linking Customers,
Process Improvement, and Financial Results*
Earl Naumann and Steven H. Hoisington

*Implementing Six Sigma: Smarter Solutions Using
Statistical Methods*
Forrest W. Breyfoggle III

The Memory Jogger Plus
Michael Brassard

*Managing Change: Practical Strategies for
Competitive Advantage*
Kari Tuominen

Improving Performance through Statistical Thinking
ASQ Statistics Division

The Desk Reference of Statistical Quality Methods
Mark L. Crossley

Six Sigma Project Management:
A Pocket Guide

Jeffrey N. Lowenthal, Ph.D.

ASQ Quality Press
Milwaukee, Wisconsin

Six Sigma Project Management: A Pocket Guide
Jeffrey N. Lowenthal, Ph.D

Library of Congress Cataloging-in-Publication Data

Lowenthal, Jeffrey N., 1958–
   Six sigma project management : a pocket guide / Jeffrey N. Lowenthal.
      p. cm.
   Includes bibliographical references and index.
   ISBN 0-87389-519-3 (alk. paper)
   1. Process control. I. Title.

 TS156.8 .L69 2001
   658.5'62—dc21   2001041229

10 9 8 7 6 5 4 3 2

ISBN 0-87389-519-3

Acquisitions Editor: Annemieke Koudstaal
Project Editor: Craig S. Powell
Production Administrator: Gretchen Trautman
Special Marketing Representative: Denise M. Cawley

ASQ Mission: The American Society for Quality advances individual,
organizational, and community excellence worldwide through learning,
quality improvement, and knowledge exchange.

Attention Bookstores, Wholesalers, Schools, and Corporations: ASQ Quality
Press books, videotapes, audiotapes, and software are available at quantity
discounts with bulk purchases for business, educational, or instructional use.
For information, please contact ASQ Quality Press at 800-248-1946, or write to
ASQ Quality Press, P.O. Box 3005, Milwaukee, WI 53201-3005.

To place orders or to request a free copy of the ASQ Quality Press Publications
Catalog, including ASQ membership information, call 800-248-1946. Visit our
Web site at www.asq.org or http://qualitypress.asq.org .

Printed in the United States of America

  Printed on acid-free paper

To Erika Gerri and Gabrielle Nomi,
my youngest daughters, for your unconditional
love, playfulness, and hugs and kisses
when they are needed most.

Table of Contents

Preface

Changing the way things are done in order to meet customer demands and increase profitability has become one of the foremost business issues of our day. In the past, change for many organizations came relatively slowly. Companies often could survive or even prosper simply by keeping their processes stable. Nowadays, however, competition in business is stronger than ever, with everyone biting at everyone else's heels. It is much more dangerous these days to complacently assume that continuing to do things the way they have been done in the past will lead to success.

As a result, both the necessity for and the rate of change in businesses large and small are increasing. More organizations are feeling the need to improve their operations wherever they can. More executives are realizing that to beat the competition, you constantly have to make things better.

And they're right. Change, if well guided and well planned, can result in new opportunities, growth, and increased profitability. This recently has become abundantly clear, as companies such as General Electric,

Motorola, and Allied Signal have made extraordinary gains by employing a change initiative known as Six Sigma.

But just what is Six Sigma?

For starters, it is very organized common sense that can lead to uncommon achievements. At its most general level, Six Sigma focuses on two things: the customer's requirements and the processes meant to fulfill those requirements. Those two factors amount to two voices: the voice of the customer and the voice of the process. Six Sigma is an initiative for getting those two voices in harmony.

That, of course, takes work. This pocket guide is about how to go about getting that work done.

The heart of the guide is its third major section, where the six-step Six Sigma methodology is presented. The six-step methodology is a road map for change, a sequential model that can be followed when deploying a sigma initiative in virtually any company. It takes you step-by-step from the point where it has become clear that there are some problems that need fixing through to the formal end of the sigma effort. In between is the selection of a project leader and a Six Sigma team, the gradual identification of one or more key processes and of a study hypothesis, the selling of a specific sigma direction to management, the sigma study itself, and implementation of the results of the study.

The first section of the guide is preparatory to the six-step methodology. This section concerns several key concepts for Six Sigma: organizations, organizational dynamics, quality, and reliability. The second section discusses the two primary human resources that are needed in a sigma effort: the blackbelt and the champion.

The final section describes how the project methodology was developed. In brief, it was based on a meta-analysis of more than two hundred projects that have been completed.

This is not a guide for the theoretician, although theory is addressed briefly, as needed. It is a practical book, a book for the practitioner charged with helping his or her organization change so as to meet customer needs more reliably and efficiently and thereby increase profits. Taken all together, this guide provides a basic understanding of Six Sigma and the tools and guidance necessary to implement it in an organization.

When I began writing this guide, my wife, Kathy, an elementary school music teacher, gave me this advice: "Keep it simple and easy to follow. Make it systematic, and your readers will understand and follow your steps." That is just what I have attempted to do. After all, step-by-step is the only way to get to where we need to go.

JEFFREY N. LOWENTHAL, PH.D.
WEST BLOOMFIELD, MICHIGAN

Section I

SETTING A FOUNDATION

Organizations and the Need for Change

Intuitively, we all seem to know what we mean when we talk about an "organization." But the word often is not as clear as we might think. If we were to ask a line manager, a senior executive, and a worker on the line to define the word, we would likely get three very different answers. One of the two main purposes of this section is to provide a working definition for the concept *organization*. The other is to explore the factors that affect organizations and require them to change.

WHAT IS AN ORGANIZATION?

From an internal viewpoint, organizations are collections of individuals. But not just any collection. Organizations are collections of individuals whose activities are coordinated. A school, for example, is more than teachers in classrooms with books and supplies. In a school, the actions of both students and teachers must be regulated and harmonized, and there must be coordination in the use of facilities, supplies, transportation, and time. Without such coordination, the school's proper product, education, cannot be produced.

Which brings us to the external viewpoint. Organizations exist within a larger environment from which they receive inputs. They also typically create outputs to the larger world since they generally come into existence to fulfill society's needs, serving as intervening elements between what society desires and the satisfaction of those desires. We need organizations to do this for us because of our individual limitations. No matter how intelligent, imaginative, or capable an individual may be, it is impossible, working entirely alone, to provide much more than the bare necessities for oneself. Countless objects and tasks require the purposeful association of individuals to enable their creation or accomplishment.

It is thus characteristic of organizations to produce a product that is desired and consumed by some portion of society beyond the organization. That product may be a concrete object, such as a toy, or a specific service, such as medical care. It also might be something less tangible, such as the education of our children produced by an elementary school or the regulation of business behavior produced by the Securities and Exchange Commission.

To complicate matters, the primary products of some organizations are not consumed by the outside world. An example of this type of organization is the Volume Mailers Association (VMA), a group of letter shop owners who meet regularly to discuss trends and new technology available to letter shops. The organization's major products are meetings, seminars, and a newsletter for its members. The consumer of these products is the

VMA itself. Still, the actions of the organization are not totally divorced from the world beyond its borders, for society has an interest in how the organization operates. For example, federal law requires that there be no collaboration for the purposes of price fixing in such organizations, so VMA members can discuss among themselves new methods in operating their businesses but not the pricing of services.

Such organizations are the exception, however, so by combining and integrating the internal and external viewpoints, let us set down the following as a reasonable definition of an organization:

> *a collection of individuals whose activities are coordinated so as to produce objects and services that society or portions of it desire and could not otherwise easily obtain.*

FACTORS THAT INFLUENCE ORGANIZATIONS

The factors that influence organizations manifest themselves internally and externally. Internal factors that affect business organizations include such items as range of products, centralization or decentralization of operations, and divestiture or acquisition of other businesses. External factors include increased competition, government regulations, and changing economic conditions. Generally speaking, all factors, whether internal or external, are interdependent. In the following sections, internal and external factors are discussed in greater detail.

Internal Factors: Anticipating Change

Every organization has two general categories of internal influence: downward pressures originating within management, and upward pressures arising from the needs and demands of the members of the organization. Downward pressures are derived from new thinking about workplace relations and business opportunities. Examples of downward pressures include management directives for centralization or restructuring of a workplace and the impact of a new product on an existing production line. Upward pressures include trade union or employee demands for more money and better working conditions and the internal enforcement of both federal and state employment labor laws.

Internal factors of organizational change present a paradox. Though the need for change may be generated at any level of the organization, the responsibility for initiating change rests primarily with management. But at the same time, management is often the guardian of established practice and the enemy of change, since change may conflict with managerial prerogatives.

The role of managers as initiators of change is less paradoxical than it seems. Only managers are equipped to take responsibility for change, and they must take that responsibility for the following reasons:

1. Senior managers are based at two knowledge levels:

   • They see the company as a whole and in its environment.

   • They have a wider range of possible models for change and have access to expert resources inside and outside the company to assist them.

2. Managers have the power to marshal resources and apply them to what they believe will benefit the company.

3. The manager's role is to make the decisions that will secure the company's well-being.

4. If changes in the company's social and political environment carry implications for the organization, it is the job of management to identify those implications and, if possible, anticipate the changes.

Managers must learn to consciously scan the internal environment for factors indicating change. Internal factors are not as readily visible as external factors, primarily because internal factors usually do not manifest themselves in a structured fashion. For example, it may not be obvious at first that there has been a shift in the educational level of employees or that there is widespread dissatisfaction among department employees concerning some key process. That is why managers must learn a special skill to deal with internal factors of change—that of consciously and purposefully scanning the internal environment for the elements of change that can be significant for the organization.

External Factors

External factors that influence organizations center on the organization's role in society. Generally, external factors are more intense and visible than internal ones and receive a more immediate response from management. Here, too, managers should consciously scan the external environment for indicators of change.

Organizations respond to external factors to maintain their internal stability. There are two general categories of external factors: government and consumerism.

Government pressures are usually less a source of anxiety to companies than is the prospect of consumer pressures. Government factors are normally steady, or at least predictable. Stability often results from the close relationship industry builds with government. The history of relations between government and industry is marked by a sequence of actions that have made the government an important player in corporate decision making. Regulations and legislation such as antitrust laws, food and packaging laws, drug safety laws, environmental laws, and automobile safety standards all represent restrictions on industry's freedom of action. They also mark points at which private industry has been made to answer to society's needs. The process of integrating government and industry will continue as society's awareness increases.

Consumerism, on the other hand, is often antagonistic toward business and provides a greater source of uncertainty. Direct actions by groups of activists to change aspects of corporate policy provide a significant new pressure for change within organizations. Such pressures represent a unique way to hold corporations accountable for the social consequences of their actions. The result has been, and will continue to be, a greater corporate sensitivity toward public concerns. For example, corporate America has increased its sensitivity to several highly visible and often politically based issues such as corporate involvement in defense industries. Even more significant is the development of consumer activist groups (for example, citizen watchdogs, community organizations, and neighborhood associations) that judge companies in areas of traditionally internal decision making. Examples of corporate scrutiny include product design and safety, as well as plant location and operation, both of which formerly have been the sacred prerogative of industry. Consumerism makes organizations more responsive to governmental and consumer influences, which shifts the role of organizations in society.

Regardless of which factor is pushing the change, the responsibility for identifying the need for change and leading the organization through it belongs to management. It is management, particularly top management, that must be sensitive to manifestations of changing conditions inside the organization and that also must scan the external environment for indicators of the need for change. Management must interpret the indicators correctly and understand where they may lead. They must then be ready to lead the organization through whatever changes are found to be necessary.

UNDERSTANDING CHANGE

Historically, change has been a slow, often painful process. In the past, whole populations that knew about certain inventions and their applications have ignored them for years, decades, even centuries. Three examples illustrate this point: gunpowder and rifle development, the printing press, and the facsimile (fax) machine.

Five hundred years passed between the first known use of gunpowder and the development of the earliest rifles in Europe. In fact, over the following three hundred years, so little progress was made in rifle development that Benjamin Franklin suggested to the Continental Congress that the new American army be equipped with the longbow because rifles were inaccurate and gunpowder was hard to obtain. ("Don't shoot until you see the whites of their eyes" was the rule to ensure that no gunpowder was wasted and that every musket shot produced a kill.) Franklin would not have had to make his recommendation if gunpowder had not been so slow in making the transition from discovery to application.

The second historical example is the printing press. Although the Arabs were aware of the technology of printing from the books of Jewish scholars and those of other religious communities under Arab rule, they made no use of the printing press until three centuries after Gutenberg's invention. Closer to the present, the facsimile machine, an indispensable tool in most organizations today, is another example of an invention whose widespread application was slow to happen. Though fax machines were invented in the 1950s, it was not until the 1980s that they became widely accepted.

In the past, change took place occasionally and irregularly. It might occur in respect to some activity in a few locations while leaving other locations untouched for long periods. Change might affect a few people in various places or large numbers in one place, but never everyone everywhere. Further, often the changes that occurred were so slow as to be virtually imperceptible. When change occurred at a faster pace, typically it was due to massive social upheavals such as foreign invasions or the overthrow of a regime.

This pattern was profoundly altered with the coming of the Industrial Revolution. The rate of change quickened in countries that became industrialized, and as time passed, more and more countries became industrialized. In the United States today, as in much of the world, the former slow pace of change has accelerated to the point where, in business, very significant changes in products and the way business is transacted can occur within a few years or even months.

Many changes are due to the rapid application of such recent inventions as global communications, the microprocessor, new plastics, and other synthetic materials. Word of new technologies and products travels quickly via professional meetings, the proliferation of scientific journals, or through the worldwide reach of television, all of which speed up the rate of change. We are getting closer and closer to the day when we will have the capability of communicating simultaneously with virtually every person on the planet Earth, and in the meantime, the rate of change continues to accelerate.

To understand change, we need to know first that there are two basic kinds of change: structural and cyclical.

Structural Change

Structural change is a fundamental transformation of an activity or institution from a previous state. After structural change, the new state is considerably different (either a rise or a decline, in some respect, from the previous state). Structural change is not reversible, and it requires permanent adjustment.

Structural change often implies radical change. For example, the speed of communications increased only slightly as messengers on horseback replaced human runners. However, the telegraph and telephone caused a dramatic change in the speed of communications.

Today, we have instantaneous communication. In the future, communications will continue to change, in speed as well as amount and format.

Again, structural change is irreversible. The thing that changes undergoes a permanent transformation and attains a new state. There may be stability in the new state, or there may be a continuing evolution to yet another new state. But there is no going back to the prior state.

The discovery of new knowledge and the creation of new technology and equipment make old knowledge obsolete. Permanent adjustment is required—if an organization does not respond, it will fall behind and be swept under by its competitors.

Structural change may require the dismantling of old institutions, relationships, and procedures and replacement of those institutions with new ones. That this must occur is understandable, as it is difficult to move successfully into the future burdened with the baggage of the past.

Cyclical Change

Cyclical change, on the other hand, is the temporary change of something from a level or state to which it is likely to return later. Over time, cyclical change tends to follow a discernible fluctuating pattern by returning regularly to a prior state. An example of cyclical change can be found in the retail industry. Every year, beginning in about late August, retailers hire additional personnel to help with the winter holiday season. This increase in hiring typically requires changes in hiring policy, training, and other administrative tasks. However, after the season is complete, the personnel roster typically returns to pre–holiday season levels.

Cyclical changes usually do not cause any irreversible alterations in the structure of the institutions or activities in which they are occurring. Cyclical changes are therefore repeating, nonstructural, and limited; and the required adjustments are temporary.

While change itself is ever increasing, becoming limitless and infinite, each type of change has its own pattern, with a discernible direction, amount, pace, and duration.

A NEED FOR CHANGE: CONTINUOUS IMPROVEMENT

Physics teaches us that for a piece of wood to burn it must be heated to a temperature at which it ignites, then burns by itself. The initial heating requires energy, but once the wood is ignited, the flame sustains itself and gives off much more energy than was required to start the fire.

A more intense fire than from burning wood can be had by igniting a mixture of aluminum powder and metal oxide. By itself, the mixture is cold and lifeless; but when heated to ignition temperature, it becomes a self-sustaining source of brilliant light and intense heat that cannot be put out by ordinary means. The mixture will burn underwater or in any other environment that would extinguish an ordinary flame. The fire is self-sustaining and does not depend on its surroundings for support.

Unfortunately, organizations do not operate like either of these examples from the physical world, as they are not totally self-sustaining but instead must rely on both

internal and external factors to succeed. In particular, the
long-term success of business organizations depends on
how well they satisfy their customers' shifting demands.
But whereas no business organization is self-sustaining,
some companies could burn with a flame more like that
of the aluminum powder and metal oxide—with a
brighter, more intense flame—if they were to dedicate
themselves to the Six Sigma ideal.

The Six Sigma initiative is based on two connected
factors: total customer satisfaction and effective and
efficient internal processes. A company's success
depends on its ability to satisfy its customers' needs and
on how well the organization's internal processes work
to meet that external demand. Therefore, the organization succeeds from the inside out. Competing from the
inside out means not merely managing employees to
make them comfortable within a company, but managing them in ways that build the firm's ability to compete
in the marketplace. The commitment and dedication of
employees to fulfilling customer needs becomes the
flame that perpetuates success.

An organization's capacity to be flexible and to
change when change is called for does not result from
quick fixes, simple programs, or management speeches.
It starts with the identification of the organization's core
competencies, which in turn guides management behavior. It includes the central realization that there is a
strong link between competitiveness, internal processes,
and effective people management. This guided management behavior then affects the attitudes and values
of both leadership and employees.

The Six Sigma process is only one method to gain a
competitive advantage. Its components are not new or

innovative—all have been around for many years, if not decades. What makes the Six Sigma process so powerful is its blending of the various components into a synergistic whole. After spending some time in the following section on the concepts of quality and reliability, you will be in a better position to understand these two concepts and how they apply to Six Sigma.

Quality, Reliability,
and Six Sigma

In talking to many professionals who have applied the Six Sigma methodology to their business processes it has become clear that that one purpose for using Six Sigma is to improve the quality of their product or service. Some others have reported that they employ Six Sigma to make their processes more reliable. Which of these—if either—is an accurate description of their goals? And what does it mean, anyway, to say that a product is a quality product or that a process is reliable? This section explores these questions and locates the two key concepts of quality and reliability in relation to the Six Sigma initiative.

WHAT IS QUALITY?

A standard dictionary definition of quality could be that which makes something what it is; characteristic element; basic nature, kind; the degree of excellence of a thing; excellence, superiority. But what does that mean? Over the years, other definitions of quality have emerged. Those definitions can be divided into several classifications—transcendent, product based, user based, manufacturing based, and value based.

Transcendent Definition

- "Quality is neither mind nor matter, but a third entity independent of the two. . . . even though quality cannot be defined, you know what it is" (R. M. Pirsig, *Zen and the Art of Motorcycle Maintenance*).

Product-Based Definition

- "The totality of features and characteristics of a product or service that bears on its ability to satisfy given needs" (American Society for Quality/ANSI).

User-Based Definitions

- "Quality is the degree to which a specific product satisfies the wants of a specific customer" (H. L. Gilmore, *Quality Progress,* June 1974).

- "In the final analysis of the marketplace, the quality of a product depends on how well it fits patterns of customer preference" (Kuehn and Day, *Harvard Business Review,* 1962).

- "Quality is fitness for use" (J. M. Juran).

Manufacturing-Based Definitions

- "Quality means conformance to requirements" (Phil Crosby, *Quality Is Free*).

- "Quality is the degree to which a specified product conforms to a design or specification" (H. L. Gilmore, *Quality Progress,* June 1974).

Value-Based Definitions

- "Quality is the degree of excellence at an acceptable price and the control of variability at an acceptable cost" (H. Broh, *Managing Quality*, 1982).

- "Quality means best for certain customer conditions. These conditions are (a) the actual use and (b) the selling price of the product" (A. Feigenbaum, *Total Quality Control*).

These definitions of quality are striking in their variety. Yet that fact in itself suggests a consistent theme, namely, that the definitions are all subjective. After all, who determines whether something satisfies given needs, or is fit for use, or satisfies certain specifications?

Suppose you received a sales order to produce a 2" × 2" × 2" paperweight. The specifications are as follows:

- Tolerance: ±0.001

- Color: Process Blue

- Materials: Steel that confirms to specification "A4"

- Delivery: Friday, 9 November 2000, between 1 and 2 P.M. EST

You work hard and produce a product that meets or exceeds all the specs. But upon delivery at 1:32 P.M. EST, your customer informs you that the product is not acceptable. You have the "proof" that you conformed to all the requirements. Is your product a quality product? According to the bulk of the definitions above, the answer is no. Though it conformed to requirements, those requirements turned out, in the end, not to be the customer's requirements. As a result, it did not meet the customer's needs.

All of this points toward a certain conclusion—that quality is a perception. And it is the customer or end user who defines what it is. The customer is the one who perceives or does not perceive quality in a product, and that perception changes from person to person. For example, at a recent training class, an attendee stated that coffee from a specific store was the highest-quality product when compared with coffee from other shops in the area. Every time she went to that store, she was assured of the same "quality product." The instructor of the course disagreed and stated that the coffee at the store the attendee liked best was no better than at any other store in the area. In the pursuant discussion, it was determined that the instructor does not drink coffee and therefore that no coffee would be considered by him to be quality coffee.

Quality is a perception. It is a mark set by a customer (sometimes consciously, sometimes unconsciously) for a product or service. A product's meeting the mark, and thus being considered a quality product, is one of the more important reasons why individuals make an initial purchase. However, for a customer to buy again and again from the same company requires something more than quality. It requires reliability. Quality may make the first sale, but reliability is what keeps the customer coming back. It is, next to quality, the most important thing to a customer.

WHAT IS RELIABILITY?

If you think about how we use the word *reliable* in everyday language, you have a pretty good hint as to what the word means. For instance, we often speak of a machine as being reliable: "I have a reliable car" or "that is the most reliable brand of lawn mower." Newspeople talk about a "usually reliable source." In both kinds of cases, the word *reliable* generally means *dependable* or *trustworthy*. In business processes, too, the term *reliable* often is used to mean dependable. But what does *dependable* mean here?

When something is dependable, there is some respect in which it does something repeatedly over time. A dependable battery is one that consistently gives you the electricity you need to start your car. A dependable news source is one that tells the truth every single time. Hitting some mark repeatedly, consistently, is the key idea behind the concept of dependability. And that's just what we mean when we call something reliable.

For example, our friend, mentioned previously, considers her source of coffee reliable because every time she buys coffee there, the coffee is good. The coffee not only hits the mark, it hits the mark consistently. And that's why she buys coffee at that store—because it is a reliable source.

Repeatability and consistency are also what we mean when we talk about the reliability of a measuring process. A reliable measuring device or process is one that gives us consistent results over and over again (assuming that the thing or process being measured is not changing). A watch is a measuring device, and a reliable watch is one that has little variability in its measurements. Now mind you, that does not mean that the watch will necessarily give the right time! Accuracy is something different. A watch that gives the correct time over and over is reliable. But if it were not reset in October when daylight savings time comes into effect, it would cease being accurate. It would start to give time one hour later than the actual time. It would still be considered reliable. It would consistently, repeatedly—that is, reliably—give time one hour later than the actual time.

Thus in measurement, accuracy is one thing, reliability another. In measurement, accuracy is analogous to what quality is for our coffee lady. She comes back to the same store over and over because the coffee she buys there repeatedly hits the mark she has established. Accuracy is like that; it's like hitting the right mark. A watch must be reliable, but it also must hit the right mark.

THE VOICE OF THE CUSTOMER

We just saw that a quality product is a product that the customer perceives as having quality. Customers may not always be able to articulate clearly just what they want in a product or service, but they usually know when they aren't getting it. For every product, every customer has a level that he or she wants that product to reach or exceed in respect to one or more of the product's characteristics. If the product reaches the desired level, the customer considers it a quality product. If it does not, the customer is likely to look elsewhere.

Other factors are relevant, too. Customers want products at affordable prices, and they want them when they want them. John may think that Company B's products are higher in quality than Company A's, but if he can't afford B's products, or if they are not available when he wants them, then he will probably settle for A's products. What customers want most, of course, are products that do all three—meet specifications, sell at a good price, and are available when requested. The company that can best provide all three is the one customers want most to buy from.

Customers want products that fit their idea of quality not just once in a while, but consistently. Remember that reliable news source talked about above? Such a source is considered reliable if he or she is perceived to speak the truth. But if we find out just once that the source has lied, then the source becomes unreliable and we will never fully trust him or her again. The same is true for products. If the store that our friend praises for its coffee fails her just once, she will never fully trust it again. As soon as it does fail, she likely will start looking around for a new—and more reliable—source of coffee to meet her standards.

The customer's desire for quality in a product actually amounts to specifications for that product. The specs may not be drawn up in a set of blueprints or a formal request. They may not even be clearly thought out by the customer. But they are specifications nonetheless. The customer's desire for reliability is simply the demand that those specs be met whenever the product is purchased. The demand that specs be fulfilled consistently is the bottom line for the customer. The phrase *bottom line* is used to describe profits. It is appropriate to point out here because the customer's demand that specs are fulfilled consistently is directly related to bottom line profitability.

Many companies do not fully realize this. They seem to realize that pleasing their customers and doing it consistently has a direct correlation to their profitability. Yet their actions often show that they are not very clear on the idea. Although they pay attention to their customers, they don't pay particularly good attention.

They don't listen closely to what their customers are telling them even though their customers are not secretive about what they want. In short, they don't pay close attention to the *voice of the customer*.

The voice of the customer has four aspects. The customer:

- demands that the product meets certain specifications (quality)
- demands that those specifications be fulfilled consistently (reliability)
- demands a reasonable price (as low as possible)
- demands that the product be available when the customer is ready to buy

Numerous feedback mechanisms can be used to determine what customers want and how well those demands are being satisfied.

SIX SIGMA AND RELIABILITY

The voice of the customer is a large part of the Six Sigma methodology. Those who undertake a sigma initiative understand that the voice of the customer is very important. The *voice of the process* is the second area of importance in a Six Sigma initiative.

The products that customers buy come from processes companies follow in production. If the product is to satisfy the customer's demands for quality and reliability, what occurs in the processes must reflect the voice of the customer. How does the process find the customer's voice?

First and foremost, the process speaks through the product itself. If defects are occurring, that is a sign that there are errors in the process. There are other types of measurements that can be made to determine how efficiently a process is working. All such measurements give a voice to the process.

Six Sigma companies are organizations that understand that the two voices, that of the customer and that of the process, must be in harmony. How is harmony accomplished? By listening closely to both voices and then acting to change the process so that it more reliably produces the products that the customer demands.

Reliability is the key. When customers receive products that do not meet their specifications, they go elsewhere. Even customers who previously have been satisfied with an organization's products, if they now purchase one defective item from the company, will be wary of the company's products in the future. And they may very well advertise their disappointment and their wariness to their colleagues.

How does a company increase reliability? How does it decrease defect rates? The general answer is that it must reduce variation in the key processes that are involved in making products. This in turn requires understanding the processes, determining how they can be improved, and implementing the changes.

That is Six Sigma in a nutshell. An organization that undertakes the Six Sigma initiative in a select area is making a commitment to intimately understand the industrial and business processes involved in that area so as to reduce variation in the processes, reduce defect rates, and more reliably meet customers' product specifications.

Six Sigma uses a measure commonly known as TDU—total defects per unit—the sum of all defective parts per million in all key steps of the process. By reducing the total defects per unit to a statistically insignificant level, a company is able to produce products that meet customer demands more reliably. The result is not only satisfied customers but also lower overall costs.

Of course, when manufacturing a product, there will always be some variation from the original design specifications. The distribution of these measurements of variation will fall on what commonly is referred to as a normal, or bell, curve (discussed in the third section of this guide). In addition to the fact that there will always be variations from the design specifications within, say, a batch, there will also be variations from batch to batch. That is because no process is perfectly centered. This variation is measured by a capability index, the Cpk, and usually falls around plus or minus 1.5 sigma. This factor also causes an increase in total defects per unit by pushing units away from the initial design value, forcing yields to go down. That is the reason the literature states that a Six Sigma process yields only 3.4 errors per million units. If you had a perfectly centered process, at the Six Sigma level, your defect yield would be 2 parts per billion compared with the shifted process, which produces a TDU of 3.4 parts per million.

Products that can be manufactured with the fewest defects and in the shortest amount of time will result in the greatest profits. A Six Sigma design process can deliver these results. Many people still fear that Six Sigma methodology is too expensive. Experience shows that when a company has the desire to manufacture with the Six Sigma process, and it plans accordingly from the beginning, costs can be kept down. As a result, companies throughout the world have saved millions of dollars using Six Sigma design.

So far the emphasis has been on Six Sigma in relation to reducing variation in processes that produce consumables. It is important to point out that sigma efforts also involve reducing not just variation but also cycle time. Six Sigma projects also can involve a process that does not produce items to be sold. For example, a sigma effort could lead to making internal processes more efficient, such as invoicing (though such a case involves products in a wider sense of the term *product* as well as customers of those products in a wider sense of the term *customer*).

In essence Six Sigma involves:

- Understanding the customer's specifications for a product and the customer's desire for reliability

- Understanding fully the processes that are involved in producing that product

- Reducing variation in those processes to increase reliability

Section three presents the six-step methodology in detail.

Section II

TWO KEY SIX SIGMA PROJECT RESOURCES

There are two players in any Six Sigma project. The *organizational champion* is the chief sponsor of the project and has the ultimate responsibility for successful completion on time and within budget. The *blackbelt* is the project leader and directs all activity in the project. In this section, I briefly outline these two key roles and further explore the topic of sigma project management.

The Six Sigma Blackbelt

A blackbelt can come from almost any specialty. When adequately trained and given technical support, blackbelts become large-scale change facilitators in the organization. They stimulate management thinking by posing new ways of doing things, challenge conventional wisdom by demonstrating successful application of new methodologies, seek out and pilot new tools, create innovative strategies, and develop others to follow in their footsteps. blackbelts can speak the language of management (for example, money, time, and organizational dynamics) as well as the language of individual contributors (for example, quality tools, statistical techniques, and problem-solving methods). They are individuals who can realize a synergistic proficiency between their discipline and Six Sigma strategies, tactics, and tools.

A successful blackbelt must be, first and foremost, a competent manager. According to the Project Management Institute (PMI) based in Houston Texas, to be successful as a project leader one must coordinate and balance nine areas of competency:

- Cost containment
- Time management
- Project scope definition
- Quality of work product
- Internal and external communication
- Human resources
- Contracts
- Office management and supplies
- Risk management

SKILL SETS OF A BLACKBELT

Management and Leadership

Blackbelts must command both the authority and the responsibility to guide large-scale projects. Project management and leadership go hand in hand. Stakeholders, team members, and the project champion expect the blackbelt to be skilled in the use of project management methods and techniques.

Decision Making

On sigma projects, countless decisions must be made. To make sound, timely decisions, the blackbelt has to have a firm grasp of all aspects of the project at all times. He or she must be able to balance costs, time, and results; prevent budget slippage and scope creep; and appropriately allocate resources if a project falls behind schedule.

Communication

Keeping others informed of activities and results can make the difference between perceived success and perceived failure of a project. The following are important areas in which the blackbelt's communication skills are needed:

- Guiding team efforts at each step of the sigma process

- Creating and maintaining work schedules

- Arranging and leading project team meetings

- Sharing project successes and results with upper management, the project champion, and other key stakeholders

Team Building and Negotiation

Blackbelts must continually build relationships among the various stakeholders: management, customers, team members, the champion, and suppliers. Power is granted only to a blackbelt who builds these relationships. An effective blackbelt must continually negotiate authority to move a project forward. That authority depends solely on his or her ability to build a strong team among internal and external players.

Planning, Scheduling, and Acting

Sigma project management consists of the same elements as in other projects. These include establishing objectives, breaking jobs into well-defined tasks, charting work sequences, scheduling, budgeting, coordinating a team, and team communications. The blackbelt must therefore be proficient in planning effectively and acting efficiently. Balancing the interrelationship between planning and scheduling is critical to project success.

Focus

Six Sigma projects may include several major activities on which different people work simultaneously. The project leader can easily get lost in the day-to-day details of specific tasks and lose sight of the big picture. Successful blackbelts jump back and forth between all facets of the identified project tasks.

Interpersonal Interaction

To be perceived as a leader, the blackbelt must be regarded as honest, capable, dependable, and personable. It is important for the blackbelt to build a positive relationship with the project champion and other key stakeholders. Effective interpersonal relationship skills are necessary to create a unified team from individuals with various backgrounds.

A BLACKBELT'S TASKS

Blackbelts lead and enjoy a high level of peer respect. They must take on considerable responsibility in managing risk, setting directions, and leading the way to breakthrough improvements. Among the blackbelt's tasks are the following:

- Leading: providing technical and managerial leadership to the sigma project team members

- Planning: determining what must be done at each step of the way, including developing a cross-functional deployment plan

- Mentoring: cultivating a network of experts in the company

- Teaching: providing formal training to personnel in new strategies and tools

- Coaching: providing one-on-one support to personnel

- Transferring: passing on new strategies and tools in the form of training, workshops, case studies, local symposia, and other communication modalities and forums

- Discovering: finding application opportunities for strategies and tools, both internal and external (for example, suppliers and customers)

- Identifying: surfacing business opportunities through partnerships with other organizations

- Influencing: selling the organization on the rise of enterprisewide integration and supporting tools

BLACKBELT TRAITS

In addition to mastering various tasks and being competent in different skill sets, there are several key traits the blackbelt, as a project manager, must possess.

Adherence to the Priorities of the Organization

Even though Six Sigma projects focus on particular processes, an effective blackbelt is most mindful of the priorities and focus of the organization. The reality of most, if not all, key organizational projects is that they should make money. Keeping the larger organizational and profit goals in focus is a key to current and future success. Even if the project does not involve a specific profit goal, the blackbelt must control the cost, time, and quality constraints of the project.

Ability to Adapt

Change will happen in the course of any sigma project. Problems will arise; adjustments will have to be made. The blackbelt must be flexible and adaptable.

Enthusiasm for the Project

Six Sigma projects can take between two weeks and five months to complete, and the process can be trying. It is crucial for the blackbelt to stay focused and to keep the enthusiasm high. The constant exhibition of focused enthusiasm by the blackbelt can help infect team members and stakeholders with the same strong, positive attitude toward the project.

The Six Sigma Champion

To succeed, a sigma initiative must have the support of the highest tiers of the organization's management. The sigma champion is the focal point for this organizational support.

CHARACTERISTICS OF THE CHAMPION

The champion is usually a member of management and is often the primary stakeholder in the area that is the focus of the sigma effort. The champion is the one most able to improve the specific process and is the one who has the most to gain if the process is improved and who feels the most pain if it fails.

There are a number of qualities that are important in the sigma champion. The champion should be experienced in organizational change and well grounded in the sigma process. The champion should have sufficient authority to make important management decisions as the sigma effort proceeds and especially as the project team confronts problems. The champion should have a robust commitment to process improvement and the success of the Six Sigma effort.

KEY TASKS OF THE SIGMA CHAMPION

Provide Vision

There are many paths from which to choose in deploying a Six Sigma effort. The principal task of the champion is to provide the vision for change and the initial direction of the sigma effort.

Develop a Strategic Project Plan

A sigma effort can consist of several smaller projects, and it is the responsibility of the champion to identify and prioritize these. Many sigma initiatives cross organizational boundaries and require strategic decisions from the champion.

Allocate Appropriate Resources and Provide Support

It is the champion's responsibility to see to it that the sigma team is given the resources it needs to carry out its functions. It is also essential for the champion to provide support to both the project leader and the team. Sigma project teams need leaders and members who are able to dedicate themselves to the project.

The champion must recruit the blackbelt and remove their day-to-day activities to provide the time required for the project. The champion should assist the blackbelt in recruiting team members and providing the time and resources needed by all involved for the project to be successful.

Remove Barriers

Sigma project teams can expect to encounter barriers. Any number of obstacles—geographic, financial, political, or personnel related—might put a sigma project in jeopardy. Alleviating these problems to allow the team to focus on its job is one of the more important duties of the champion.

Summary

Of course, everyone involved—from the highest levels of management to the members of the project team—has an important role to play in a sigma effort. The blackbelt and the champion, each in his or her own way, are the leaders. The rest of the project will take direction from these two roles.

Section III

THE CRITICAL SIX

The six-step sigma methodology is a model that can be used by any business to bring about measured, evidence-based changes in key industrial and commercial processes. Such changes are geared toward increasing customer satisfaction, reducing costs, and building profits. The six major steps constitute a holistic approach to identifying crucial issues of process redesign—leading you from the point of identifying a problem to the completion of the change process.

In this section, the step-by-step approach to the six-step sigma methodology is described.

A Broader
Six Sigma Methodology

The six-step model covers more ground than other sigma methodologies currently on the market. First, this methodology begins with the identification of a problem or issue—a crucial step in any reasoned change process. There are many ways of identifying a problem, but not all ways of doing so will also serve to point toward a solution. To recognize that profits are down, for example, is one form of problem identification. Stating the problem in such general terms does not suggest a direction for resolving the issue. What is needed is a finer definition of the situation, one that will suggest a productive way of dealing with the problem. In its first step, the six-step methodology focuses on identifying the problem or issue in such a way that steps to solution are evident.

A second unique aspect of this methodology is in step 4, the selling of a proposed solution to management. Though it is assumed that senior management will support exploring the sigma project at the very outset, that support will likely be taking place *before* the problem or change issue has been defined well enough to

allow a particular course of action to be recommended—
and thus before senior management knows the cost of
change. Once the problem or issue has been more
clearly specified and the sigma team has devised a set
of specific recommendations for dealing with it, senior
management must be resold on the sigma project.
Specifically, they must be sold on the value of the particular solution offered by the team.

THE CRITICAL SIX

Step 1—Identification

In identifying the problem or issue to be studied, attempt
to keep the scope manageable. Determine whether
the issue can be addressed effectively in two weeks
to five months.

Step 2—Laying a Foundation

The first step in laying the foundation is to determine
where internal reviews and approvals are needed. In
addition, step 2 lays a research foundation that will serve
to begin outlining the direction for change. This step
also provides methods to identify, assess, and map particular business processes and offers the necessary
framework for providing insights into the process being
explored and translating them into actions leading to
process redesign and refinement. Here again, the six-
step methodology is different from other Six Sigma
methods inasmuch as step 2 employs two complemen-
tary mapping approaches—flowcharting and integrated

flow diagramming—as well as a review of cultural considerations. At the end of step 2 you should be able to develop your initial hypothesis.

Step 3—MECE

MECE (pronounced "me-see") stands for *mutually exclusive, collectively exhaustive*. It is a helpful term that has been used in the literature on management. Its pedigree stems from logic and set theory.

The disciplined application of the MECE principle will determine the issues surrounding a problem and provide crucial keys for devising a solution. MECE helps to refine the initial hypothesis generated by step 2 and to ensure that all issues of relevance are covered and covered only once. When this step is completed, the project team can be confident that it has grasped all the important aspects of the issue or problem and can identify and develop the associated study components.

Step 4—Selling a Solution to Management

Nothing gets done until something is sold to the decision makers. In this case, what must be sold is the sigma plan (the solution) to senior management. Full buy-in from management is required in order for the project to progress successfully.

Step 5—Designing, Verifying, and Implementing the Six Sigma Study

Step 5 employs all the data collected to develop and implement the study. Three stages—design, verification, and implementation—are used to define the project methodology, verify project progress against the hypothesis, and fully implement the improvement plan.

Step 6—Closing the Project

The findings of the study are shared with those who have the greatest interest in its success and results— the key stakeholders. What makes step 6 significant is that though it may constitute the closing of one project, it should lead to a wider effort within the company to implement the findings of the study.

As you can see from the chart in Figure 1, the model includes decision points and revisiting previous steps. The constant refinement of the study makes this six-step model unique.

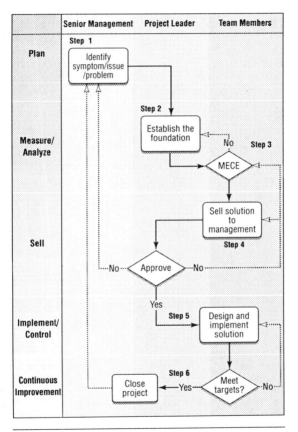

Figure 1 High-level methodology.

Step 1:
Identify the Symptom or Issue

The first step in the six-step methodology is the preparatory phase. Step 1 consists of five sub-steps, beginning with choosing one issue or problem to address through the sigma initiative and ending with the selection of team members (see Figure 2). In between, the project leader is identified, a preliminary situational analysis is undertaken, and the scope of the project is determined.

First, consider the preconditions for any sigma effort to take place. Six Sigma offers powerful tools that can bring about significant change in an organization. Senior management must set the stage before a sigma change initiative can begin to take root in an organization. This requires the convergence of several factors. First, key people in top management must be convinced that change is needed in the organization. Second, those same individuals must believe that initiating a sigma process to identify and investigate possible directions for change is worth doing. This, in turn, requires that they become aware of the various steps of the Six Sigma process and the potential impact of that process on the organization's structure, culture, and resources. The

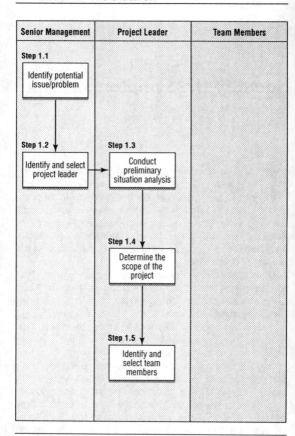

| Senior Management | Project Leader | Team Members |

Step 1.1

Identify potential issue/problem

Step 1.2

Identify and select project leader

Step 1.3

Conduct preliminary situation analysis

Step 1.4

Determine the scope of the project

Step 1.5

Identify and select team members

Figure 2   Step 1: Identify the symptom or issue.

third factor is that these same individuals must act on their beliefs.

Much of the work of setting the stage will be done by the Six Sigma Steering Committee (3SC), which should be established at the start of the sigma process. The 3SC is a high-level management group whose charter and focus is to guide the direction of the change process. The committee's purpose is to ensure that Six Sigma projects receive the attention, focused support, and participation of the highest management levels in the organization. The sigma champion will be part of this group.

Specifically, the 3SC has the following responsibilities:

1. To guide and direct the initial steps of the Six Sigma process.

2. To ensure appropriate resource allocation and support for Six Sigma projects.

3. To maintain the focus of Six Sigma efforts on the organization's core competencies and on meeting or exceeding customer requirements. Note: A proper focus should not be on profit per se, as profit will flow naturally from targeting ways to better serve customers by doing, more efficiently and effectively, the things the organization does best.

4. To establish guidelines to resolve interdepartmental problems. The Six Sigma Steering Committee should seek to anticipate the possibility of interdepartmental or interdivisional conflicts arising as a result of implementing a change initiative, and should devise and communicate guidelines to help ensure that everyone involved is working toward the same goal.

In fulfilling these responsibilities, the 3SC will need to focus on a number of issues at various stages of the Six Sigma change initiative. The 3SC is involved in the following tasks:

- *Developing and maintaining the 3SC organization charter.* The 3SC organization charter should be clearly defined. The charter will help guide the committee's own work and provide direction for the entire sigma process.

- *Identifying any organizational constraints, "burning issues," and key opportunities.* This is the beginning of the ongoing process of clearly defining the issues that offer opportunities for organizational change.

- *Educating the organization about Six Sigma and why the initiative is being undertaken.* Everyone in the organization who will be affected needs to know what to expect from the initiative, as well as the rough timelines.

- *Devising and communicating the rewards and benefits of Six Sigma.* This, of course, is one of the important keys for leading personnel to fully embrace the sigma initiative.

- *Coordinating the Six Sigma methodology throughout the organization.* What gets done first, second, and third must be coordinated among all involved staff and departments if Six Sigma is to be enacted with maximum efficiency.

- *Determining metrics to measure gains that are achieved through the Six Sigma process.*

- *Collecting, analyzing, and distributing project results throughout the organization.* This is another of the central communications functions to be overseen by the 3SC to ensure that all involved parties are apprised of what is happening.

- *Adapting Six Sigma project results into ongoing strategic and operational planning.* It will be the 3SC's responsibility to make sure that this all-important matter of follow-through is accomplished.

The steering committee is integral to the success of the Six Sigma initiative from problem identification through implementation and closure.

STEP 1.1—IDENTIFY AND SELECT POTENTIAL ISSUES OR PROBLEMS

The main role of the 3SC is to identify potential issues or problems. Numerous sources of information can be used to identify Six Sigma projects.

Customer Feedback

The term *customer* is used in the broad sense, referring to whoever is the user of the product or service that is generated by following a process. The customer for a finished automobile or magazine is the person who buys the item. These are customers external to the process. There are also internal customers. For example, the user, and thus the customer, of an automobile's side mirror at a certain point on the assembly line is the person charged with installing it on the automobile frame. The customer for a bundle of pages at a magazine bindery is the individual who jogs the pages to even them out before feeding them into a stitching machine. The customer for a form that is filled out by employees in the service departments at a number of store locations may be personnel working in the data entry facilities at a centralized geographic location. The recipient at each of the points in a process is a customer. For most business processes, in fact, we can identify a number of internal customers, typically one or more for each major step of the process.

Both external and internal customers can be characterized by their needs. Internal customer needs include the adequate completion of the previous step in the process. That previous step should produce a product—whether an automobile side mirror, a bundle of magazine pages, or a completed form—that enables the internal customer to do his or her job correctly.

Persistent negative customer feedback about a product from either external or internal users is an important source of information about the functionality of a process. Complaints from consumers or other external customers signal a problem somewhere in the entire process of developing, manufacturing, and shipping the product to the user. Where the product and need are internal, negative feedback is a signal to examine that part of the process preceding the point of complaint. Opportunities for improvement arise as more becomes understood of internal and external customer needs and how well the needs are being fulfilled. The blackbelt should review the current mechanisms used to assess customer requirements, including how information is fed back to the 3SC for resolution.

Internal Suffering

Most people want to take pride in their jobs. Whether they are involved in making a car, a golf ball, or a report, they want to perceive themselves as helping to create a quality product in an efficient manner. When that is not happening, employees often become disgruntled, edgy, or just plain unhappy. The people involved in a process are generally the ones who know best whether it is working well. If people are unhappy with the way things are being done, that issue should be noted and investigated. Talking to the people who are intimately involved with the process and taking their feedback seriously can provide crucial information about problems that need to be addressed.

Outside Opportunities

Benchmark data may allow management to compare and contrast different opportunities not previously considered. Such information can suggest new markets for old products, new products, or even new lines of business.

An Objective Vantage Point

Those directly involved in a process may be the best ones to determine whether the process is working well. But it is also true that in many cases an objective vantage point can offer new insights into the way a process or area does, should, and could work. A manager, or some other employee, may be able to pinpoint problems by taking an objective, comprehensive overview of the issue.

That insight can provide a reason to recognize an opportunity for process redesign. But once such an opportunity has been recognized, management needs to ask and attempt to answer pertinent questions relating to both the process and the opportunity:

1. How and why did an interest in improvement arise?

2. What are the particular areas of concern?

3. What products or services does the process produce?

4. Who is the customer of the process (consumers, the next department, some other company, and so on)?

5. What are the customer's needs?

6. What form of feedback is available about customer satisfaction, and what does the feedback indicate?

7. Is it necessary to improve the process because of newly established goals or objectives?

8. Is the problem cross-functional? If so, will there be a need to form cross-functional teams to resolve it?

9. Is there anything to compare the process with and model it after? Is this process comparable to others within or outside the organization?

Such questions help to identify areas, issues, or points of interest and suggest opportunities for improvement. Which issue should be the primary focus? Is it possible to work on more than one at a time? Which will provide maximum benefit? These questions should be asked at the outset. To help devise solutions, it is necessary to prioritize each opportunity. Doing so will help determine which opportunities would be most beneficial and whether there are natural pairings that can be addressed at the same time. Several criteria may be used as guides in the prioritization process:

Recurring problems. The existence of recurring problems that stem from a particular process constitutes a reason to consider making redesign of that process a priority.

Level of performance. Comparing current performance to a benchmark may provide enough evidence to make improvement of a process a priority.

Company objectives or goals. Priority can be given to processes that affect the accomplishment of present or future business plans.

Impact on company resources. Resources that are not being used effectively or workloads that are out of balance can constitute sufficient reason to make redesign of the process a priority.

Using these and/or other internal company criteria, the 3SC must choose from the issues that have been introduced. Initial projects should be small, manageable efforts where the methodology can be applied successfully. Larger efforts should be tackled once participants feel comfortable with the six steps and the tasks associated with completion of a project.

Once the focus of the sigma initiative has been determined, the next step is to select the blackbelt. If more than one project has been selected for a sigma initiative, it may be necessary to select a blackbelt for each. This will depend on how closely related the issues are and the extent and difficulty of the identified projects.

STEP 1.2—SELECT THE BLACKBELT

The 3SC or the sigma champion needs to select the blackbelt. This decision is based on the individual's interpersonal skills and previous experience leading continuous improvement or change initiatives.

Once selected, the blackbelt is briefed on the issue or problem and provided with the general direction of the sigma project. From here it is the blackbelt's responsibility to determine the specific project's direction.

STEP 1.3—CONDUCT A PRELIMINARY SITUATIONAL ANALYSIS

This step is carried out by the blackbelt and consists of several substeps (see Figure 3). The emphasis is on preliminary analysis. It is not until step 3.7, determining the hypothesis, that the sigma team gets a clear focus on a process, including the relevant variables. Step 3.1 is the first effort to map out the direction that may be taken in the overall project.

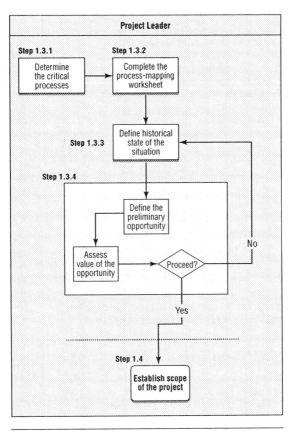

Figure 3   Step 1.3: Conduct a preliminary situational analysis.

Step 1.3.1—Determine the Critical Processes

Determining the critical processes is the most important activity in step 1. While selecting a project for Six Sigma, the 3SC will have identified, in a broad sense, one or more high-level processes considered to be centrally involved in the issue. The blackbelt refines the critical processes involved in the issue or problem.

A restatement of how the process can more efficiently meet customer needs and demands is made at this time. Review the answers to the questions that were addressed in step 1.1. In addition, ask the following:

- What products or service does the process produce?

- Who is the customer?

- What form of feedback is available to measure customer satisfaction?

At this point only preliminary answers can be expected to the questions. When the Six Sigma team is formed, the questions will be answered in depth.

Step 1.3.2—Complete a Process-Mapping Worksheet for Each Critical Process

The process-mapping worksheet provides an executive summary of the process in a consolidated format. In completing the worksheet, the blackbelt is required to focus on the process itself and how it relates to what is critical to the customer. The form is completed sequentially, using all material collected up to this point. It may not be possible, at this stage of the initiative, to provide more than cursory information for some of the sections.

Once completed, the document should be shared and discussed with members of the 3SC. Following is a review of the worksheet sections.

Section A—Process Inputs

Process inputs are the equipment, materials, methods, and environment necessary to produce the products and services.

Section B—Process Outputs

Process outputs are the products or services produced.

Section C—Specific Process Targets

This section defines the objectives, goals, and targets that the organization feels are acceptable for the process.

Section D—Voice of the Process

The voice of the process is the feedback mechanism by which the quality of the process is measured and examined against specific targets or metrics. It consists of measurements of process outputs taken over time compared with targets, thereby indicating the actual performance levels of the process.

The voice of the process should mirror the voice of the customer. To properly identify and understand the voice of the process, the following seven questions should be answered as well as possible at this stage:

1. What critical characteristics of the process can be improved so that the products and services will meet or exceed the customer's needs and expectations?

2. What targets (improvements) should be established so that the critical characteristics will meet or exceed the customer's needs and expectations?

3. What additional information is needed to define those targets?

4. What should be measured inside or during the process?

5. Is there a system for collecting information on the performance of the process?

6. Do the measurements being used to assess the voice of the process reflect the voice of the customer?

7. Is the process currently meeting the established targets for the critical characteristics of the process?

Section E—Catalyst Event

The catalyst event is the event that signals the beginning of the process and thus forms its initial boundary. The catalyst event might be something as simple as the placement of an order or a calendar event.

Section F—Customer

Customers are the users of the products or services produced by the process and are the ultimate judges of the quality of the process outputs. At this point, the primary customer should be identified. The primary customer is the most important customer for the specific product or service, the principal reason the process exists, and the end boundary of the process.

Section G—Customer Needs and Expectations

This section illustrates the attributes of the products and services that customers require. Material for this section can be obtained from the process sponsor or stakeholders.

Section H—Specific Customer Targets

Specific customer targets translate customer needs and expectations into specific, quantifiable attributes that can be used to assess the quality of the product or service.

Section I—Voice of the Customer

The voice of the customer is the feedback mechanism by which customers' satisfaction with the product or service is measured and examined. To properly identify and understand the voice of the customer, the blackbelt must answer the following three questions:

1. How well does the process satisfy customers?

2. What means are in place to find out whether customers' needs and expectations are being met?

3. Do the measures being used adequately assess the voice of the customer?

Several techniques are available to assess the voice of the customer:

Surveys. This is a basic way of extracting feedback from customers through questions directly related to the product or service.

Interviews. Interviews are more effective than surveys for gathering detailed answers to questions. Interviews use open-ended questions and allow interviewees to answer questions in more detail.

Benchmarking. This method of determining customer satisfaction requires the company's product or service to be compared with a best-in-class competitor's product or service. By measuring customer satisfaction with the competitor's product, one's own product can be rated accordingly.

In measuring customer satisfaction, it is important to create a feedback mechanism (survey, interview, and so forth) that can be used repeatedly. This provides consistency over time, which is important to validate continuous improvement in the process. There is a time lag in gathering the voice of the customer. To help compensate for that problem, the voice of the process, which is the reflection of the voice of the customer, must be measured continually throughout the sigma effort.

Step 1.3.3—Define the Historical State of the Situation

At this point, the process stakeholders have been identified and many have been interviewed to obtain their perspective and input on the proposed project. It is important to understand any history behind the issue. How long has the issue or problem been going on?

Step 1.3.4—Assess the Potential Opportunity and Return on Investment

Once the critical processes have been identified, it is crucial to decide if an opportunity exists. An opportunity may not exist for the following reasons:

- An inability to agree on the voice of the customer(s)

- A lack of needed involvement by process sponsors (see the next heading for a definition of the process sponsor)

- Unreasonable timing expectations

- Inability to resolve important questions relating to the process

- Conflicting interests due to multiple sponsors

- Low return on investment or little value added to the company

If any of these obstacles exists, it can be assumed that a sigma effort will be headed for difficulty. You may need to redefine the opportunity or end the project at this point.

Orient the Process Sponsor

The process sponsor is the person who either owns the process or is responsible for the successful operation of the process. The process sponsor is typically the liaison between the sigma team and the process stakeholders. If the sponsor is willing to address the opportunity, there must be an understanding of the rationale for initiating the Six Sigma effort. This will help in determining what goals the sponsor believes must be achieved to ensure the project's success. In addition, the sponsor should articulate the perceived problem and what effect the Six Sigma effort will have on customer satisfaction. This builds ownership of the design effort and increases the success and durability of any process improvement.

Define the Preliminary Opportunity

Next, it is important to gain agreement between the process sponsor and the blackbelt on a number of issues:

- Who are the process customers? Is there a primary customer, or do several customers have an equal stake in the process?

- What is the process output in terms of products and/or services? What type or types of transformation (physical, location, or transactional) occur within the process?

- What is the current level of customer satisfaction with the process output? Do the customers have any particular concern, such as quality of the output or price? How is customer satisfaction being measured?

- Are there any performance data that can help in the evaluation of the process's current performance?

- What are the perceived constraints of the process?

- Finally, how does this process compare with similar processes in other organizations, internal and external?

Assess the feasibility of proceeding with the sigma project by reviewing the answers with the 3SC and project sponsor.

Assess the Value of the Opportunity

Once it has been determined that an opportunity exists, the 3SC must decide whether the benefits outweigh the costs of change. The 3SC will assess whether the increases in efficiency, effectiveness, and adaptability exceed the cost of the resources the sigma effort will consume. Addressing the following questions can assess the value of the opportunity:

1. Who would benefit most from improving this process?

2. Which people have an interest in the performance of the process?

3. Would those people recognize the value and priority of the effort?

4. Would improvements in the process increase the competitiveness (in terms of increased market share, throughput, quality, or profitability) of the organization?

The fourth question is the most important in determining whether the Six Sigma effort should be undertaken. If a significant benefit is not realized from the effort, the process should not be targeted at that time.

STEP 1.4—DETERMINE THE SCOPE OF THE PROJECT

The focus of this step is on establishing boundaries of the sigma process and clarification of project goals. Both boundaries and goals are based on current assumptions about the existing process and are subject to change with the attainment of more input, analyses, feedback on progress, and viewpoints.

This stage consists of five substeps (see Figure 4). The first is to identify and involve process stakeholders. This is essential to accurately determine the scope of the project. Additional tasks to be accomplished during this step include the following:

- Create valid assumptions about the process, and communicate those assumptions to all others involved with the project to ensure acceptance and support.

- Design a work team for the project.

- Develop tentative strategies about how to do the work, allowing room for modifications as time progresses.

- Outline an agreement between all stakeholders in and promoters of the process change initiative.

Step 1.4.1—Identify Stakeholders

Process stakeholders are those persons who are most able and willing to improve the process. They are typically members of management and have the most to gain if the process is improved and will feel the most pain if it is not. They may include people from both inside and outside the organization. For example, the set of stakeholders could include a representative from an outside supplier of inputs to the process or from an external organization that is a consumer of the product produced by the process. At this point, the key stakeholders should be identified and involved in the Six Sigma effort.

Once the stakeholders have been identified, the blackbelt involves them in helping to determine the initial

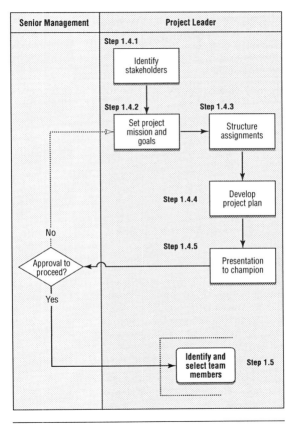

Figure 4 Step 1.4: Determine scope of the project.

assumptions for the project. Assumptions should be discussed and well understood by the blackbelt and the champion and relayed to the stakeholders for input. To clarify project assumptions, the following questions should be addressed:

- What resources are available to carry out process improvement?

- What are the benefits and the drawbacks of a project such as this?

- Why is Six Sigma being introduced, and is this the right time to do the project?

- Has everything, including future plans, been considered?

- Do you have the availability and are stakeholders ready to commit to the project?

Step 1.4.2—Set Project Mission and Goals

The blackbelt must define the project mission and set attainable goals. The initial boundaries of the sigma project also must be determined. A review of all previously collected data, including reviewing the answers to questions already asked, will provide a framework to use to refine the mission and goals. In order to refine the project mission and goals the blackbelt must know the following:

- Who is the primary customer and what are the products/services that the process delivers?

- What are the inputs to the process (for example, people, methods, material, equipment, environment)?

- What are the perceived boundaries of the process?

- Which organizations are included within the boundaries?

- Is the project manageable given these boundaries?

- Are there any potential problems or challenges to using these boundaries?

After the boundaries have been identified, the blackbelt will develop a statement of the project mission and goals. The purpose of the mission statement is to formalize the direction and purpose of the project. A clear statement of project goals will provide stakeholders and team members a clear path to accomplish the project.

Step 1.4.3—Structure the Assignments

The blackbelt next outlines the potential assignments for future team members. The team members have not been selected at this point. The blackbelt is determining the skill types that will be needed among members and the probable size of the team.

Step 1.4.4—Develop a Preliminary Project Plan

In this step, the blackbelt develops an initial plan of action for presentation to the 3SC. The project plan should include:

- the tasks to be performed during the sigma effort

- the skill sets and numbers of individuals who will be responsible for those tasks

- the individuals who will assist or support

- the estimated time for completing the tasks.

Step 1.4.5—Present Project Plan to the Champion and Formalize a Contract

The project plan should be presented to the champion. In the event that approval to proceed is not received, the project leader may return to step 1.4.2 to rethink and reset project limitations and goals or start from the beginning and refine the project plan.

When the champion accepts the project plan, a formal contract should be developed that contains the signatures of the blackbelt, the stakeholder or stakeholders, and the process sponsor or sponsors. The contract should reflect agreement among its signees and should include:

- project assumptions and goals

- division of work, including tasks and assignments such as data collection, data analysis, and meeting preparation

- the review process by senior management

- logistics, including frequency of meetings, length of the process, requirements of team members, and review points by stakeholders

- formal recognition of the efforts of team members (for example, build into performance objectives, discuss at business review meetings).

STEP 1.5—SELECT TEAM MEMBERS

Selecting the right members to form an effective team is critical to the success of the project. The team should include members familiar with all points in the process. Members should include representatives from each of the following:

- The customers who receive activities within the process—both internal and external
- The areas that perform activities within the process
- The supplier or suppliers who provide input to the process

Members are assigned to the team according to their skill and role in the organization. While a stakeholder may initiate an individual's inclusion on the team, the member's participation requires the full support of management. Without support, priority conflicts are likely to adversely affect the team's progress.

The following criteria should be considered in the selection of team members:

- Knowledge of the process
- Interest in process improvement
- Creativity and problem-solving ability
- Knowledge of quality tools
- Leadership ability

Leadership ability is important for all members because each member will be working not only with the rest of the team but also within the organization. Team members should possess a number of other skills to be effective, including the following:

- Data collection and analysis

- Documentation, including procedure writing and requirements and measurements

- Communication and persuasion, including conflict resolution, written and oral presentations, and meeting facilitation

- Quality improvement and measurement tools, including problem solving, basic quality tools, and statistical techniques

With the selection of the sigma team, the first step of the Six Sigma process has been completed.

Step 2:
Establish a Foundation

The champion and blackbelt have established a base for the project, and core team members have been selected. Establishing the foundation for the project is step 2.

Team members will work independently or in small groups of two or three. Working independently maximizes coverage and ensures that all aspects of the issue at hand are explored. Any area that is overlooked will become evident when establishing the foundation.

There are five main substeps to be carried out in the second stage of the six-step methodology (see Figure 5). The substeps lay the foundation for the sigma effort by providing the basic research that will guide later stages of the process.

STEP 2.1—ORIENT THE TEAM

At the team orientation—a meeting that can be expected to last from one to three hours—all data collected in step 1 are shared with the team members. Members

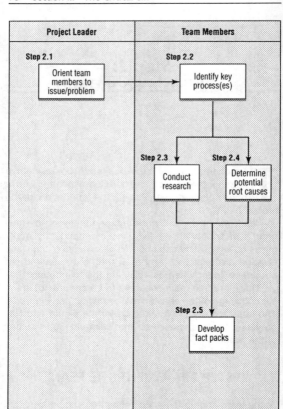

Figure 5 Step 2: Establish a foundation.

should be provided the material prior to the meeting to give them time to develop questions and comments.

STEP 2.2—IDENTIFY KEY PROCESSES

Team members examine the material from step 1.3, conducting a situational analysis, and determine the key processes involved in each area of concern. The processes are then assigned to different individuals or groups. Each team member is responsible for conducting research relevant to the assigned process.

STEP 2.3—CONDUCT RESEARCH

This step comprises four activities—flowcharting, integrated flow diagramming, process constraint analysis, and cultural factors analysis (see Figure 6). These four tools allow team members to look at a process from four different viewpoints: decision points, communication paths, obstacles, and people issues.

Step 2.3.1—Flowchart Each Process

It is important for the entire team to understand the basic structure of each process. When there is a common understanding of what is involved in the process the team can agree on where improvements can be made. One of the better ways to help generate this common understanding is by creating a flowchart that graphically represents the sequence of activities in the process. A

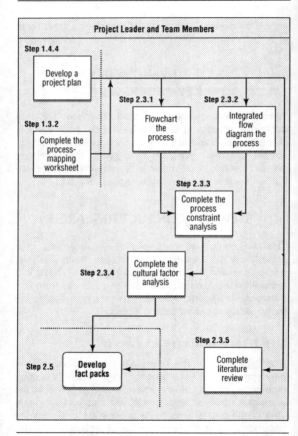

Figure 6 Step 2.3: Conduct research.

graphic description generally can be grasped more quickly than a written procedure because it represents a great deal of information in relatively few symbols.

A process control diagram should be created to provide an overview of process flow—including inputs, outputs, and customers. The process control diagram will show which organizations (for example, departments, suppliers, and customers) fit into the process and how they are linked, and it will help in pinpointing just where problems arise within the process. In creating this overview, the team will be able to confirm or to change the project scope (step 1.4) and boundaries that were determined.

Flowcharts should be completed for at least two, and possibly three, levels of the process. Level-1 flowcharts define the key activities in the process at the macro level. The level-1 flowchart will comprise several groups of activities and reflect the principal transformations between groupings. Several activities are contained within a single rectangle at this level and will not contain sufficient detail to identify process-enhancement opportunities.

A level-2 flowchart displays activities at the next level of detail using the level-1 chart as a guide. At this point, however, the team must distinguish between an activity and a task. A task is the most basic unit in the process hierarchy, while an activity consists of several tasks linked together. A level-2 flowchart will display the process with enough detail to pinpoint specific opportunities.

A level-3 flowchart displays the process at the task level only. A level-3 flowchart may be necessary when the level-2 flowchart does not lend itself to analysis, but level-2 charts are usually sufficient to identify specific opportunities. Once the level-2 flowchart is complete, activities can be mapped at the task level if necessary.

Step 2.3.2—Create an Integrated Flow Diagram for Each Process

An integrated flow diagram (IFD) is a graphic representation of the physical and communication patterns of a process. An IFD is made up of four basic elements— pipelines, activities, files, and external entities (see Figure 7).

The symbols and method used to complete an IFD are adapted from the systems analysis technique called data flow diagramming. There are two styles for depicting data flow: the Yourdon-DeMarco style and the Gane and Sarson style. The principal differences between the IFD and the data flow diagram involve their application and scope. For example, data flow diagrams were designed for data processing applications, whereas the IFD can be used for any business process. While both data flow diagrams and IFDs show information flows, IFDs also display the flow of physical products through the process.

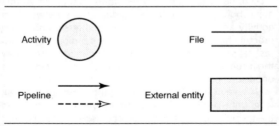

Figure 7   The four elements of an integrated flow diagram.

Pipelines

A pipeline moves a single package of information or material between the activities, files, and external entities shown on the IFD. It is symbolized by a named vector or arrow to show the interface. The following is a useful set of conventions for dealing with pipelines:

- No two pipelines have the same name.

- Names are chosen to represent not only the package that moves over the pipeline but also what is known about the package.

- Pipelines that move into and out of files do not require names; the file name will suffice to describe the pipeline. All other pipelines must be named.

Thin, thick, and broken lines can be used to distinguish between types of pipelines, but the IFD's creator may apply a variety of conventions to these. The thick-line vector often represents a flow of physical materials from point to point, such as the movement of tape from a storage facility to a tape silo. The thin-line vector often is used to represent the flow of information—such as reports or telephone calls—between activities. Some IFD creators use the thick line to show the principal flow, or main manufacturing pipelines, while using thin lines to represent support pipelines (for example, scheduling and production control).

Two other points are worth noting here. First, you should be careful not to attempt to represent pipeline control points on the IFD, as such items should be represented on the flowchart. Second, if a pipeline cannot be named easily, it is probably not defined adequately.

Either several packages are being transmitted along the pipeline, or an incomplete package is being transmitted.

Activities

Activities represent some amount of work performed on a package. A common convention is to represent activities by circles on the IFD, though ovals sometimes are used. Either way, make sure to give the represented activity a name that clearly and accurately describes the activity. Each activity should be numbered, with the numbering convention depending on how the various diagrams interrelate.

Files

A file is a collection of information or material, or a space where this information or material is stored. For an IFD, a file is any temporary repository for information or material. Examples of files for information are computer tapes, a specific area on a computer disk, a card data set, an index file, or an address book. Files for material include, for example, loading docks, warehouses, racks in warehouses, and even wastebaskets (the circular file). A double straight line often represents a file, with the file's name in close proximity. Since the IFD must be meaningful to its users, file names also need to be clear and meaningful. Avoid using coded names or abbreviations for files, and be sure not to give the same name to two files on a single IFD.

External Entities

Any process can be described on an IFD with pipelines, activities, and files. An IFD is clarified and becomes more useful when the process is shown in the larger context of external entities. An external entity is a person or organization outside the boundary of the process that is a net originator or receiver of the process being mapped. The key qualifier here is the phrase "outside the boundary of the process." A person or organization inside the boundaries is characterized by an activity on the IFD.

By convention, external entities are represented by named boxes, with pipelines flowing into and/or out of a single box. Boxes should be used sparingly on the IFD, and they should not represent major concerns. External entity boxes exist only to provide commentary about the process's connection to the outside world. If a box represents a major concern in an IFD, the boundaries of the process are probably not defined correctly.

An example of an IFD appears in Figure 8.

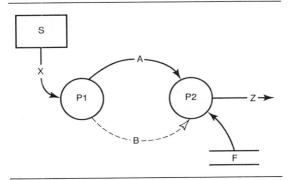

Figure 8   An integrated flow diagram.

Step 2.3.3—Complete the Process Constraint Analysis for Each Process

A process constraint analysis is a brief examination of those obstacles that prevent a process from satisfying the customer or from operating effectively and efficiently. The process constraint analysis worksheet can be used to organize the findings.

To begin the analysis, the team should identify any obstacles that prevent the employees who are part of the process from doing their work properly. The best source of information is the employees themselves. Simply ask them what, if anything, prevents them from doing their job correctly. After listening to the answers, the team needs to identify, as precisely as possible, where and why the constraints are occurring.

The sigma team must decide if a particular constraint is a true constraint or a self-imposed one. A true constraint is often a physical constraint that needs capital improvements to overcome, such as the size of a room or building, the capacity of a particular machine, or a necessary piece of new equipment. Some true constraints, however, are not physical. For example, a law or regulation that requires the organization to perform (or not perform) certain types of activities is a true constraint. In contrast, a self-imposed constraint is one that the organization imposes upon itself and that typically can be removed without any major capital outlay. Examples include employee dress codes, approval signatures, and internal rules and policies. Organizational structure or functional/departmental structure also may represent self-imposed constraints. The team cannot overcome a process constraint without knowing where and why it exists, but to pinpoint the constraint can require critical thinking, as its presence may not be obvious.

Step 2.3.4—Complete the Cultural Factors Analysis

Up to this point, the team will have made progress in understanding the mechanics of the processes. Cultural factors, those factors that involve people, may affect a process and also need to be understood. For example, if the individuals involved with the process feel that they have little or no control over their work environment, that is likely to be the source of problems. On the other hand, too much control also can lead to difficulties. Feelings of control or lack of control spring from the culture of an organization. Without a cultural factors analysis, the sigma team may eventually find that redesigning the process reduces positive cultural factors or introduces new negative ones, either of which can generate new problems and put success of the sigma effort in jeopardy.

In the 1950s, Fred Emery and Eric Trist defined six factors common to all studies of culture and employee motivation. These factors directly correlate with commitment, high productivity, and lower absenteeism and turnover. They fall into two sets—optimum factors and maximal factors.

Optimum Factors

According to Emery and Trist, the first three factors—empowerment, variety of task, and feedback/learning—occur at a specific optimum level in organizations (that is, a process may have too much or too little of that particular factor).

Empowerment

Individuals are empowered to the degree that they can make decisions that affect their work environment. These include controlling time, schedule, materials, and work pace. If employees have little sense of empowerment, they feel controlled or imposed upon. If the employee has too much empowerment, the result can be chaos and confusion. For example, without realizing their impact, employees with too much empowerment may make sweeping decisions that affect other departments or organizations. While employees should be empowered, that empowerment should have limits.

Variety of Task

Variety of task involves the issue of specialization. The path of specialization has led many American businesses down a road that perhaps seemed smooth and profitable for a time but eventually became fraught with troubles. By reducing each activity to many small, redundant tasks (the foundation of traditional manufacturing) and thereby creating a lack of variety for the employees performing those tasks, a business runs a risk of creating boredom and reducing job motivation, both of which increase errors. On the other hand, too much variety can lead to confusion and employee paralysis. As with empowerment, seek a balance. Each employee should have a sufficient variety of tasks to promote interest, but a limit on this variety is needed to eliminate anxiety and confusion.

Feedback/Learning

The feedback/learning factor concerns both the timeliness and the amount of data regarding goals achievement that an employee receives from management. Too much feedback and close supervision (standing over an employee's shoulder) can cause overload and low morale. Too little feedback, however, makes it possible for an employee to repeatedly fail. Again, look for the golden mean: enough feedback should be given to promote self-control and learning, but not so much as to overpower the employee. Such feedback should be built into the task wherever possible.

Maximal Factors

Maximal factors are those that organizations can have too little of, but never too much.

Mutual Support and Respect

Creating an environment of mutual support and respect between management and employees is critical for process success. Where support and respect by management are high, employees feel valued and perceive few or no barriers regarding levels, status, and opportunities. But when support and respect are low, the employee tends to feel subservient and looked down upon, with both morale and performance suffering as a result.

The Big Picture

Employees want and need to know how their work contributes to the whole: they want to see the big picture. Those who do not know the impact of their actions on the processes downstream from them are less likely to care than those who do. Educating employees about where in the big picture their actions fit tends to provide them with a fuller sense of place and greater pride in knowing the importance of their work.

Career Pathing

All employees need to know that there is opportunity for growth within the organization. Each employee must continue to learn and have the opportunity to move to other jobs, departments, and divisions. If a career path is not available, the employee may leave the organization or "internally retire." An employee who has internally retired does just enough work to get by. Employees who lack job motivation and job satisfaction are an obstacle to the success of the process, not to mention the company.

Step 2.3.5—Complete a Literature Review for Each Process

So far the research has been on one or more internal processes. In conducting a literature review, team members step outside the processes. The review of literature can itself be considered both a process and a product. As a process, it amounts to the act of surveying all relevant information related to a specific topic. As a product, it is the written report that summarizes information within the context of a research study.

A comprehensive and effective review of the literature will cover prior research relevant to the process and serve to stimulate new ideas among team members. There are five types of review:

1. Context reviews place a specific project in the big picture.

2. Historical reviews trace the development of an issue over time.

3. Theoretical reviews compare how different theories address an issue.

4. Methodological reviews point out how methodology varies by study.

5. Integrative reviews summarize what is known at a point in time.

STEP 2.4—DETERMINE POTENTIAL ROOT CAUSES

Using the data that have been collected in the course of the previous steps, team members should attempt at this stage to determine potential root causes for the problem or issue under investigation. A helpful procedure to go through in determining root causes is to ask three levels of *why*. For example, suppose we ask, initially, "Why is *X* happening?" Our answer may be, "Because of *A*." If so, our next question should be this: "Why is *A* happening?" If the answer to that question is "Because of *B*," then we should ask, at the third level, "Why is *B* happening?" In practice, the procedure is not always as simple as it appears here, but it often is an excellent way for investigators to find themselves quickly focused on the most critical aspects of some process that has gone awry and that needs to be understood as clearly as possible.

It should be emphasized that the team is still at an early stage of analysis here, so whatever answer is given to the question "What is the root cause?" is preliminary. It will not be until the next step that the closest analysis of the process will take place. It is still important to try to answer the question as fully as possible at this point, as the answers given here are an important preparation for step 3, MECE.

STEP 2.5—DEVELOP FACT PACKS

A substantial amount of information has been collected on the process or processes of interest. Processes have been mapped using several different tools. Background information has been collected. A cultural factors analysis has been conducted, and related literature has been reviewed. Now each team unit dealing with a particular process—a single team member or a small group—should review all data that have been obtained about the process, arrange them in a logical sequence, and prepare a "fact pack"—typically a report—detailing what has been found.

These fact packs are the culmination of all the research conducted in step 2, establishing the foundation. Once all the steps have been completed, the team is ready to move to step 3, MECE.

Step 3: MECE

The core research for the problem or issue has been completed and the sigma team is ready to move forward with the project. The job is to distill the information collected and categorize the material so that it is MECE—mutually exclusive and collectively exhaustive. Once the blackbelt and the team are confident that all aspects have been reviewed thoroughly, the next step is to design the study to improve the process under investigation (see Figure 9).

STEP 3.1—REVIEW FACT PACKS

Every member of the team should review all the fact packs that were prepared at the conclusion of the last stage. The information contained in the fact packs will be crucial to completing the next two steps—determining the initial hypotheses and identifying the key drivers.

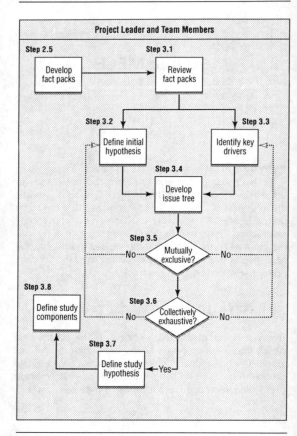

Figure 9   Step 3: MECE.

STEP 3.2—DETERMINE THE INITIAL HYPOTHESES

Because the fact packs are likely to contain plenty of information, team members may feel that the issue or problem confronting them is overly complex or even unsolvable. As the team sifts through, discusses, and digests the information and reviews the root cause of the problem (step 2.4), the key factors affecting the issue will come to the forefront. As a result, the team will be able to develop a set of initial hypotheses related to solving or alleviating the problem.

It is possible that at this point the group as a whole will decide on a single hypothesis. It is more likely that the team will generate differing ideas about which factors are the more important ones to be concerned with. Each hypothesis put forward will be a proposed problem-solving map based on the research that was carried out in step 2.

STEP 3.3—IDENTIFY THE KEY DRIVERS

While developing a hypothesis, team members should identify what they consider to be the key drivers. Key drivers are those factors that have the greatest impact on the problem or issue. Many elements can affect a process at the point where a problem resides. Identifying the key drivers requires digging down to the core of the problem, focusing in on the select few factors that have the most impact, and ignoring the balance.

Determining the key drivers goes hand in hand with developing initial hypotheses, as there is likely to be one or more initial hypotheses for each key driver.

STEP 3.4—DEVELOP AN ISSUE TREE

Once the initial hypothesis has been developed and the key drivers identified, the team should create an issue tree. Simply stated, this is done by setting down each key driver identified at step 3.3 as a main branch arising out of the issue. Factors that relate to each key driver are then set down on the issue tree as branches off of the main branches. This process may continue down to three or more levels.

Figure 10 provides an illustration of an issue tree that might be constructed for the problem of increasing production throughput for a company. Three main branches are shown: reducing waste, product design, and increasing sales. These are the key drivers, the factors that the team has identified as having the greatest impact on production throughput. Each main branch, in turn, has two or three subbranches that represent factors that affect the key drivers, with further branching from each of these. This process continues until the critical factors affecting the issue have been determined for each key driver.

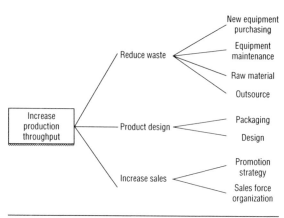

Figure 10   An issue tree.

STEPS 3.5 AND 3.6—MECE, MUTUALLY EXCLUSIVE AND COLLECTIVELY EXHAUSTIVE

MECE is a formula intended to structure the team's thinking with maximum clarity. While the "ME" and the "CE" parts are listed as two separate steps, in practice they are completed simultaneously.

To apply MECE, the team needs to take a hard look at the issue tree and ask two questions. First, are the factors or issues listed distinct from one another, or do they overlap? If the answer is that each is independent of all others on the tree, then the issues can be considered mutually exclusive.

The team should ask whether every aspect of the problem is covered by one and only one of the issues presented. The team should question whether they have thought of everything. If the answer to that question is yes, then the branches on the issue tree can be considered collectively exhaustive. If the answer is no, then the team should return to steps 3.2 and 3.3 to determine any additional key drivers and to further develop the initial hypotheses. The team should revise the issue tree as needed until all key drivers have been identified, making sure that the issues and factors on the revised issue tree remain mutually exclusive.

The importance of making sure the issue tree is MECE cannot be overstated. Clear thinking in solving business problems is like clear thinking in solving problems in science. Both begin with an exhaustive categorization of the subject matter. That is what MECE is all about—categorizing the issues distinctly so they are seen clearly.

STEP 3.7—DETERMINE THE STUDY HYPOTHESIS

The anatomy of the problem and what effects the various issues have on the problem have been laid out in the form of the issue tree. That problem has been examined and reexamined to make sure that it is MECE—that all the parts are there and that every part is in its proper place. During this process, new insights into the issue were gained; one or more of the initial hypotheses may have been altered or rejected and one or more added.

At the end of this process the team may be convinced that there are several processes that affect the problem or issue. The team may believe that several cogent hypotheses and several studies could be done whose results might be important for dealing with the issue. However, at this time it must narrow these possibilities down to one or in some cases, a few specific study hypotheses. Though considerations of time and cost may come into play in choosing the study hypothesis, it is most essential that the team choose a hypothesis that has two characteristics:

1. Given the evidence collected and the analysis made so far, the hypothesis is likely true; and

2. If the hypothesis is corroborated by the study, significant process improvement can very likely follow as a result.

The study hypothesis will concern a specific process that has been identified by the team as playing a key role in the issue or problem. In the next step, this process will be broken down further into its essential factors.

STEP 3.8—DEFINE THE STUDY'S COMPONENTS

With the study hypothesis chosen, the study's components must be determined. This process consists of two substeps: defining the variables and specifying the measurement system and data vehicles (see Figure 11).

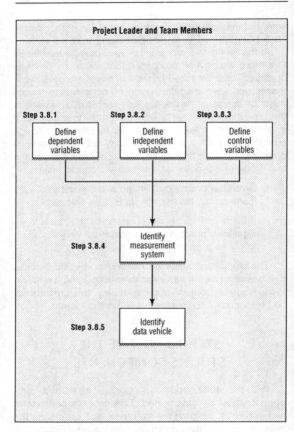

Figure 11   Step 3.8: Define the study's components.

Step 3.8.1—Define the Variables

A variable is a quantity that can take on any value within some range. Everyday examples of variables are temperature, the price of a gallon of milk, and the time it takes to drive from home to work. Variables can be contrasted with constants, which—as the name implies—are quantities that remain the same over time or vary so little that their variation is considered inconsequential. Whereas the time it takes to drive from your home to your place of work is a variable, the distance from your home to your place of work is a constant.

The value of a variable will depend on the value of other variables. For example, the time it takes you to drive to work in the morning will vary depending on (among other things) the condition of the road. Since drive time depends on road condition, it can be considered a *dependent variable* in this context.

If we stick with our example, we can see that clearly, the condition of the road does not depend on drive time (the relation is the other way around). Being independent of drive time, road condition can thus be considered an *independent variable* in relation to drive time. Of course, that's not to say that road condition is independent of all other variables. Because the condition of the road depends on the state of the weather, road condition is a dependent variable with respect to weather.

The Six Sigma team must identify the dependent variables in the process under investigation. The dependent variables will be those that are the presumed effects of the other (independent) variables. Thus they will be the ones that can be predicted by knowing the values of those other variables. A relationship diagram that identifies the dependent variables should be constructed to help specify them as clearly and fully as possible. Once defined, each dependent variable should be examined to determine its unique properties, as well as both its constraining and desirable characteristics.

The independent variables must likewise be identified. To identify the independent variables—those that determine the values of the dependent ones—it helps to construct a cause-and-effect diagram showing which factors affect the values of the dependent variables. Once identified, those factors will constitute the set of independent variables.

Having identified the dependent and independent variables, the Six Sigma team is two-thirds of the way toward determining the critical components of the process. All that is left to do is to determine the control variables.

Control variables are independent variables that are chosen to be controlled in the Six Sigma study. They are selected for control to determine more clearly just how they affect the process and/or what values they can be given to maximize process efficiency. In choosing the control variables, it is important for the team to ensure that control objectives are clearly defined.

Step 3.8.2—Identify the Measurement System and Data Vehicles

With key variables identified, measurement scales and methods of measurement must be formulated for each variable. Both of these, scales and methods, must be defined to ensure that the data gathered will be precise. If measurements are made on too rough of a scale, valuable information will be lost.

Other decisions related to measurements also have to be made. How often and by whom will the measurements be made, and what tools will be used? How will the gathered data be recorded, transmitted, and stored for future analysis? These are all important questions that deserve well-thought-out answers. The success of the sigma effort depends on the reliability of the data-gathering procedures.

With the measurement system and data vehicles determined, step 3 is complete. Guided by the research results from step 2, the sigma team has analyzed the issue to the point where a specific study hypothesis and direction for the proposed study has been chosen.

At this point it is only a *proposed study*. The blackbelt and the team must now convince senior management to give the go-ahead to implement the study.

Step 4: Sell the Solution to Management

This step is the key decision point for the Six Sigma process. Most or all costs have been in soft dollars, that is, labor and time. Step 4 contains a great deal of activity and may have a significant impact on the organization, including substantial cost in time and material.

It is the purpose of this step to gain the approval of senior management for proceeding with the project. To gain that approval, the team should prepare for and make a formal presentation to all stakeholders. This process can be broken down into four parts: creating the presentation logic, creating supporting charts, prewiring the presentation, and giving the presentation itself (see Figure 12).

STEP 4.1—CREATE PRESENTATION LOGIC

In steps 2 and 3, the team covered a good deal of ground in significant detail. In preparing for the presentation, it is important not to get lost in those details.

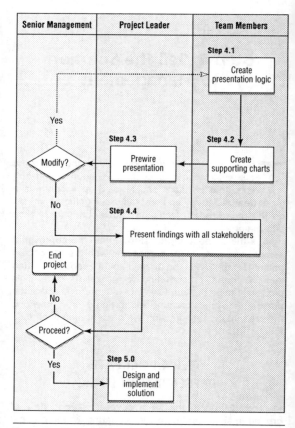

Figure 12 Step 4: Sell the solution to management.

If the team has done its job well, it will be able to offer strong reasons in support of its choice of study direction, and wherever there are strong reasons, those reasons can be set out in clear, logical structure. That is what the team should be striving for in developing the presentation—a logical structure that will be clearly evident to the stakeholders. A certain degree of salesmanship is good to bring to the presentation, but if the reasoning that the team has used to get to its conclusion is sound, and if that reasoning is presented simply and lucidly, it will speak for itself.

STEP 4.2—CREATE SUPPORTING CHARTS

Charts and other visual materials help make a presentation lively and can give punch to ideas and make them clear. Too many details in the form of charts can hinder the clear flow of ideas. The team should be clear on the specific purpose of each piece of supporting material and how it will help get the crucial ideas across to the audience.

STEP 4.3—PREWIRE THE PRESENTATION

Prewiring the presentation simply amounts to providing the crucial information to attendees before the formal meeting occurs. A good presentation should contain nothing new for those present. Accordingly, the black-belt should lead each of the key stakeholders through

PHASE ONE: DESIGN THE STUDY

Step 5.1—Determine and Set Specifications for Critical-to-Process Characteristics

Refer to Figure 13 for a chart of steps 5.1 through 5.6. Critical-to-process (CtP) characteristics are those factors, aside from the study's control variables, that could have a significant impact on the process itself or the validity of the study and that must themselves be controlled so as to fall within certain parameters. For example, the team might determine that only assembly line A should be used for the study since line B is too often down. Once the CtP characteristics are determined, their specifications must be set.

Step 5.2—Create a Verification Plan

The verification plan will identify specific, measurable indicators of process improvement. It is through the measurement of such indicators that the process will find its voice during the study. The team must again address, and give detailed answers to, the questions of what is to be measured during the study, including how, when, and by whom.

In answering these questions, the process aspects that act as a substitute for the demands of the customers will be identified. During previous steps, care should have been taken to determine the voice of the customer. Customers often make only general demands, and it is at this point that generalities are translated into specifics of process output that can be monitored during the pilot. These specific measures will comprise the current voice of the process.

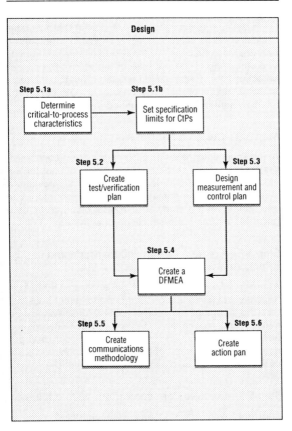

Figure 13 Step 5: Design the study—phase one.

In defining the measures, it is crucial that the team is clear about its objectives. They should be stated using operational definitions. This will help ensure a complete understanding of the purpose of the study. The overall objective should address the question "What is the team trying to accomplish?" The answer should match the improvement opportunity identified in step 1.

Step 5.3—Design a Control Plan

At the same time the verification plan is being completed, the team should also be creating a control plan for the study. The control plan is a document that provides a step-by-step written summary of the actions required at each phase of the study. The control plan serves as a guide to determine the sequence of activities.

Step 5.4—Create a Design Failure Mode and Effects Analysis

A design failure mode and effects analysis (DFMEA) is an analytical technique ensuring, to the extent possible, that the potential failure modes and their associated causes and mechanisms have been considered and addressed. Information for the DFMEA is obtained primarily from the content of the control plan, though parts of the verification plan also may be pertinent.

Step 5.5—Create a Communications Methodology

The most well-designed and well-conducted study is useless if its findings are not properly communicated to others. This step requires the team to establish a plan for how and when implementation information will be shared, and with whom. Multiple methods of communication should be considered—newsletters, town hall meetings, video—whatever methods will most thoroughly and accurately disseminate the information.

Step 5.6—Create an Action Plan

At this step, assignments are made to specific persons. The roles and responsibilities of participating individuals are specified in the action plan, along with the timing of each task.

PHASE TWO: VERIFICATION

Step 5.7—Conduct the Pilot Study

Refer to Figure 14 for a chart of steps 5.7 through 5.10. The pilot study will be conducted as a scaled-down version of the business process on which the team has chosen to focus. The general objective is to determine whether varying certain process factors (the control variables) will result in an improvement in overall process performance as measured by the dependent variables.

In conducting the pilot study, conditions (other than those in the control variables) should deviate as little as possible from ordinary process conditions. If the study does diverge in some respect from actual conditions, that should be taken into account in such a way that the validity of the study results are not jeopardized.

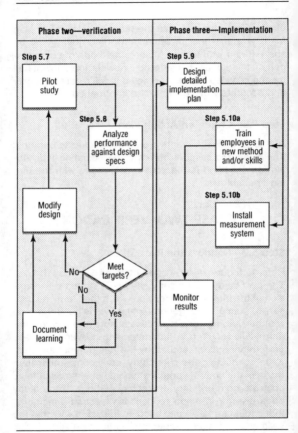

Figure 14 Step 5: Design the study—phases two and three.

Step 5.8—Evaluate Study Results

In evaluating the study, it is important for the team to make accurate and fair comparisons with the old process. Both analysis of the gathered data and feedback from customers should be used to determine whether the altered process met target objectives. Thus the following questions should be answered to determine the success of the study:

- *Do the data support a statistical conclusion that there is improvement in the process?* If there is an improvement, it is important to demonstrate it statistically to ensure that it is not the result of a chance variation.

- *Does the customer perceive an improvement in the goods or service?* Although focusing on the indicators (the voice of the process) is necessary, it is not sufficient to ensure high quality. Quality is the perception of the customer. To ensure that the changes made to the process during the study actually did what they were designed to do, it is crucial to attend to the voice of the customer.

The team needs to verify the results over a long enough time to ensure that the changed process is stable and that any gains will continue into the future. Both the voice of the process and that of the customer should be queried continually during the entire length of the study.

If results of the pilot study show that changes have improved the process as predicted, then those results should be communicated to the organization, and the next step—implementation—can begin. If not, the team must return to the design phase, rethink the design of the study, and modify the study's variables as necessary.

PHASE THREE: IMPLEMENTATION

Step 5.9—Design an Implementation Plan

With the study's success comes the opportunity for the team to devise the plan that will allow process changes to be made on a large scale. This implementation plan will encompass all organizations involved in managing and operating the process.

To create a common understanding of what is to be done, the team should begin by defining a set of implementation objectives. These should be extensions of the objectives set for the study and should encompass what is happening, why it is happening, and what will result. Since the crucial aspect of these objectives is their specificity, operational definitions should be used throughout.

For multiorganization projects, the team should do each of the following in developing the implementation plan:

- Determine who will be affected by the changes and in what way

- Make sure involved individuals in each organization know what the goals of the project are, what has to be done to achieve those goals, and who is charged with ensuring that the necessary actions to accomplish the goals are performed on time and with precision

- Develop a device that can be used to organize the implementation of changes and measure progress

In a multiorganization project, the team may encounter conflicting interests, with one organization's actions negatively affecting another organization. This cannot always be avoided or even fully corrected. Articulating the shared goals of the organization will help the team make unbiased decisions. As an aid in doing this, the team can use a technique called *shared objectives and overlapping plans of action*. This technique, which is useful for any level of conflict, consists of three steps:

1. Establish goals shared by all members of the team.

2. Determine the individual objectives of each organization represented on the team and involved with the project and make sure that those objectives are supportive of the overall goal.

3. Decide how much support each organization needs from the others in order to accomplish its own objectives.

Once the team decides on a course of action, all time constraints and task interdependencies should be incorporated into the plan. This can be done with the use of a project management system such as the critical path method or the program evaluation and review technique.

The final aspect of developing the implementation plan is the creation of a control plan. The control plan will specify ways of measuring the process after changes have been made, to ensure that process improvements are maintained over time. These measures will be taken from the verification plan that was developed in step 5.2 and used for the study. The measures should be in-process measures rather than the stored data used for the study so as to provide current information to those running the process.

When the implementation plan is complete, the team should review it with the champion, the stakeholders, and others who will be involved in implementation. This review should include the following:

- How implementation will go through the project management system

- How implementation will be monitored by the control plan

- Which changes are needed in the environment and in personnel

- Where potential problems may arise and the precautionary measures that were designed to solve those problems

STEP 5.10—EXECUTE CHANGES

The final stage of step 5 is to execute the implementation plan. The champion and stakeholders are the ones responsible for overseeing implementation.

Commitments have been made and must be kept to ensure effective implementation and timely flow of action items. Problems will inevitably arise. These may be relatively minor, such as a need for additional equipment or extra training, or they may call for more comprehensive changes. Whenever changes are necessary, the implementation plan should be updated accordingly.

It is important that everyone involved remember that the primary goal of implementing the changes is to improve customer satisfaction. Therefore, the stakeholders, the champion, the team members, and the blackbelt should all continue to keep the customers' opinions at the forefront and be prepared to make the necessary adjustments to the change process to ensure continued customer satisfaction.

With the completion of the study and the implementation of its results, the sigma project is complete. The final step is to formally close the project. If the sigma effort has been successful, this last step in the six-step methodology is liable to be a particularly sweet one.

Step 6: Close the Study

At the close of the sigma project, a formal presentation should be made of the team's findings, with study results and implementation details presented to all stakeholders. The process can be broken into parts similar to those in step 4, selling the solution to management, (see Figure 15).

STEPS 6.1 AND 6.2—CREATE PRESENTATION LOGIC AND ILLUSTRATIVE MATERIAL

Designing a clear presentation involves finding the proper balance between detail and main points. The champion and the blackbelt may choose just to explain the study results and implementation as well as highlight how the Six Sigma process worked from beginning to end. Showing how the methodology was used to bring about a successful conclusion may help build support for other sigma efforts. The use of supporting charts and

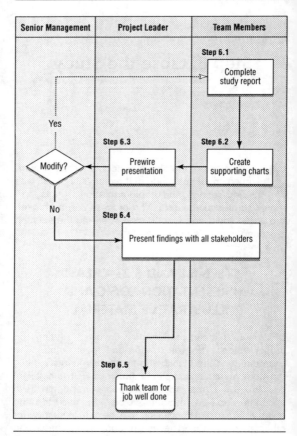

Figure 15   Step 6: Close the study.

other illustrative material should be chosen to enhance the presentation, not to overwhelm the audience.

STEP 6.3—PREWIRE
THE PRESENTATION

As in step 4—selling the solution to management—the blackbelt should lead each of the key stakeholders through the presentation beforehand. This will enable specific questions or concerns to be aired in a casual atmosphere and any feedback from individual stakeholders can then be integrated into the presentation.

STEP 6.4—PRESENT FINDINGS TO
ALL STAKEHOLDERS

If the previous steps have been taken, there should be no surprises for anyone at the formal presentation, and the talk should go smoothly. With everyone present already apprised of the ideas being presented and thus working from a shared knowledge base, discussion is likely to be positive and lively.

STEP 6.5—THANK THE
TEAM MEMBERS

Both the champion and the blackbelt should thank each team member for his or her participation.

Summary

The six-step methodology begins with a set of problems calling for attention. It is often unclear where focus should be placed. The methodology leads the blackbelt to choose a specific problem and clarify the factors affecting the issue. The blackbelt is able to devise a hypothesis for improving a key process involved in the issue. The hypothesis is put to the test in a study, improvements are identified, and the solution is implemented. With a show of appreciation to the team, the sigma process is formally closed (though, of course, implementation continues).

It's easy.

But of course we all know that it is not quite that easy in practice. Each step and substep takes time, and obstacles arise that must be overcome.

Still, the way is smoother with a plan in hand that gives the blackbelt a good idea of what should be done at each stage. Though conducting an actual sigma effort is certainly not as easy as reading about the six-step methodology, putting that methodology to work in practice should make the effort easier—and more fruitful.

How This Methodology Was Developed

Over the past few years, the methodology documented in this pocket guide has been presented at several conferences and to peer groups. One key question often arises: "How was the approach developed?"

The foundation was established initially in September 1999. This author originally received a commission to examine the curricula of various Six Sigma training programs available on the market. Funding was provided by an automotive original equipment manufacturer (OEM). Prior to the start of the study, additional funding was received from an insurance provider, a healthcare system, and a petroleum refinery.

With the funding, 40 companies that were "implementing" Six Sigma were identified. The purpose was to examine operational Six Sigma, design for Six Sigma, entry and operational skill sets of practitioners, and deployment characteristics. Within these 40 companies, 270 projects were identified. Key personnel at the companies were asked to define what made the project either a success or a failure. Along with attempting to achieve a Six Sigma level of defect rate, meeting or exceeding project targets within budget and with a minimum of organizational conflict were identified as success or failure factors.

Key leadership identified those projects they considered to be successes or failures (based on the criteria outlined above). Documentation of these projects was reviewed and the data categorized. In addition, approximately 195 individuals within these companies were interviewed. Interviewees included the project leader (that is, blackbelt or greenbelt), team members, and customers.

With the project and interview data categorized, the information was analyzed using three methodologies: front-end analysis (Ron Zemke); performance technology (Joe Harless); and instructional systems design (Ron Mager, Walter Dick, and James Carrie). When that analysis had been completed, an overview methodology emerged. Further reviews and analysis by various professionals from a variety of professions (such as, quality, business, finance, organizational development, operations management) helped solidify the final approach outlined in the prior sections.

Index